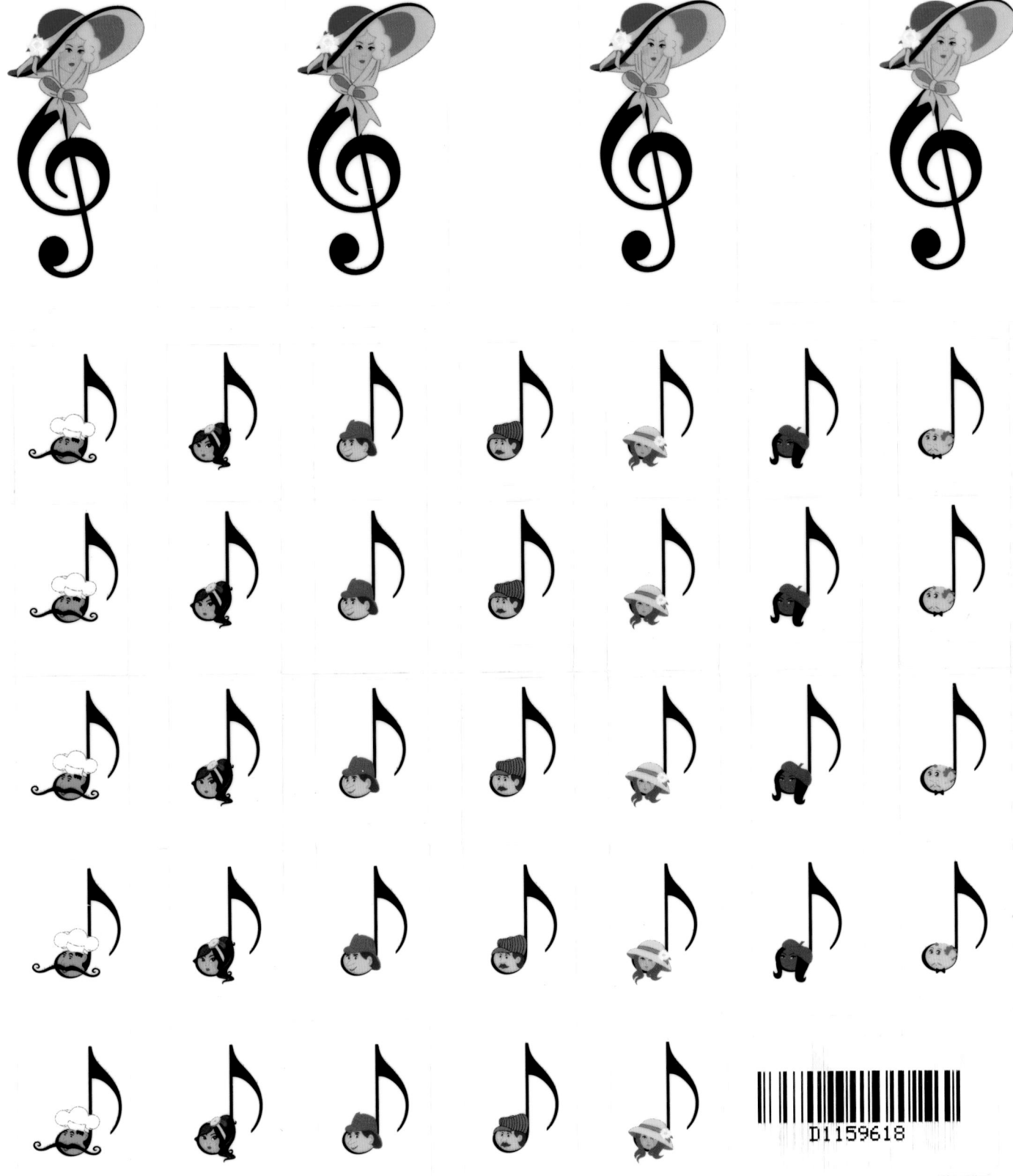

First published in 2009 by Simply Read Books
www.simplyreadbooks.com

Library and Archives Canada Cataloguing in Publication

Biklou, Eliyana
        Lady Treble and the seven notes / Eliyana Biklou, author and
illustrator. – 1st ed.

ISBN 978-1-897476-21-5

        1. Musical notation – Juvenile literature. 2. Music theory – Juvenile
literature. I. Title.

MT7.B418 2009   j781   C2009-901953-1

We gratefully acknowledge for their financial support of our publishing program the Canada Council for the Arts, the BC Arts Council, and the Government of Canada through the Book Publishing Industry Development Program (BPIDP).

Book design by Natasha Kanji

10 9 8 7 6 5 4 3 2 1

Manufactured by Hung Hing Printing Group
Manufactured in Shenzhen, Guangdong, China, in October 2009
Job # SR0904001

Lady Treble
& the seven notes

Written & illustrated by Eliyana Biklou

Simply Read Books

It's fun to look
at Carlos the Cook,
who's sipping a shake
and grilling a steak.

When work is done,
he sings for fun.
We all agree
his note is "C."

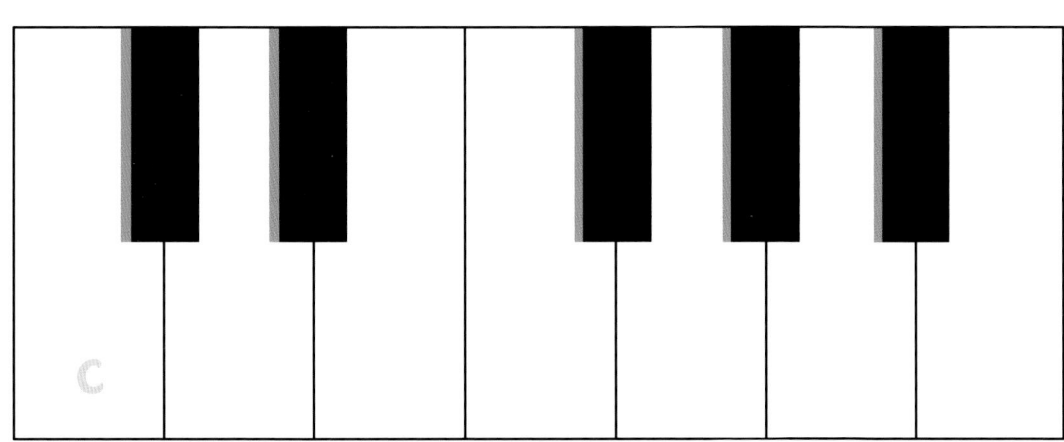

Hum "C" and stick the note on the right key!

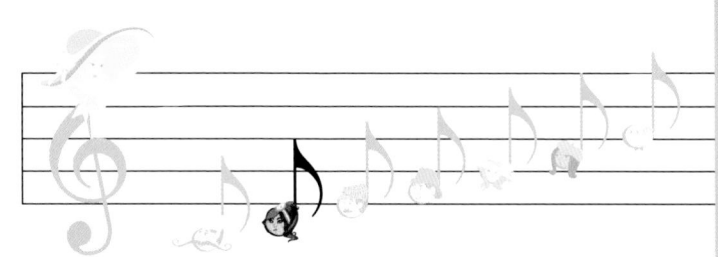

"An apple a day
keeps the sniffles away,"
says Donna the Doc,
who loves to rock.

When work is done,
she sings for fun.
We all agree
her note is "D."

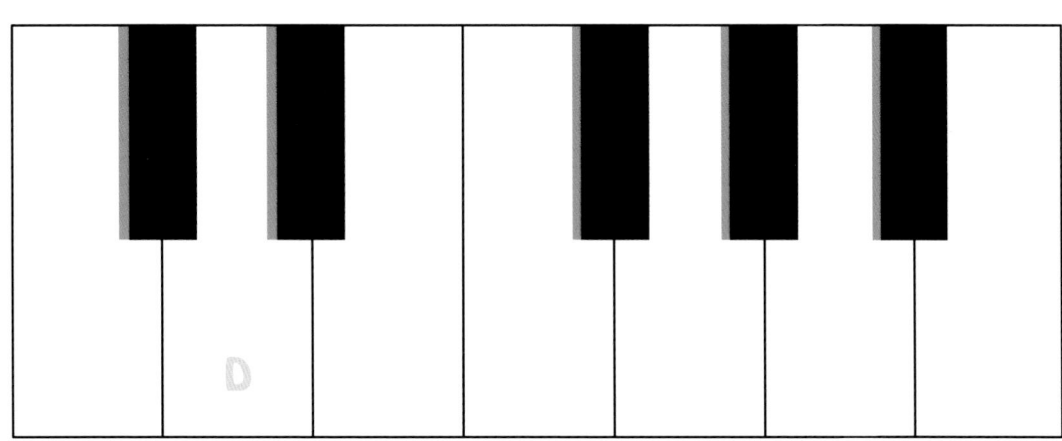

Hum "D" and stick the note on the right key!

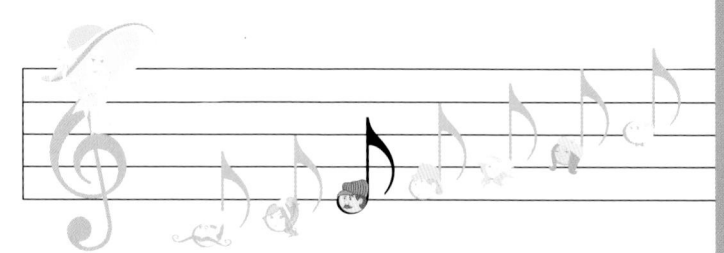

Ed Engineer
has no fear.
He drives his train
through snow and rain.

When work is done,
he sings for fun.
We all agree
his note is "E."

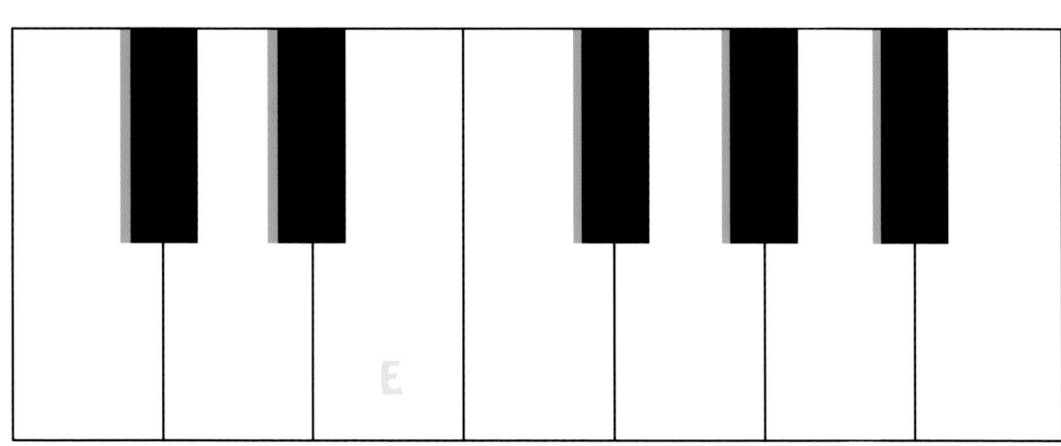

Hum "E" and stick the note on the right key!

Fireman Freddy
is always ready.
He never tires
of fighting fires.

When work is done,
he sings for fun.
With "E" to the left,
his note is "F."

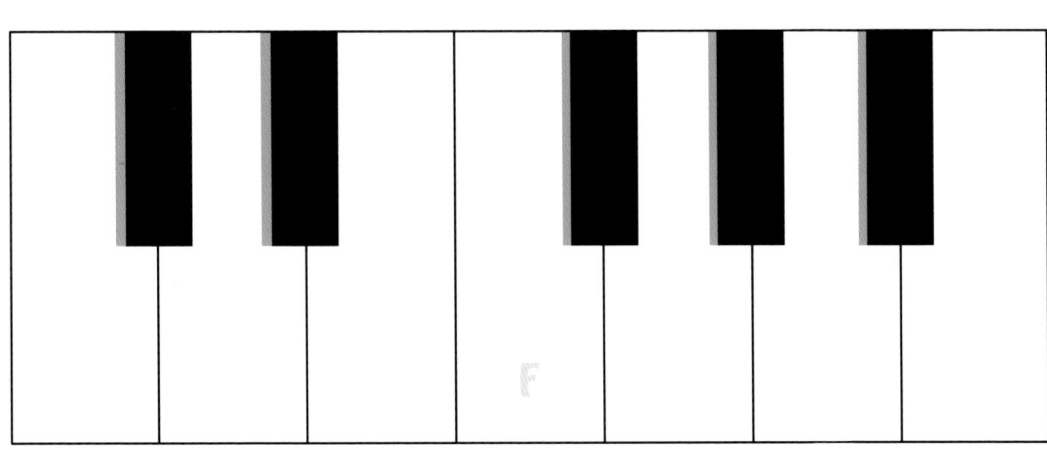

Hum "F" and stick the note on the right key!

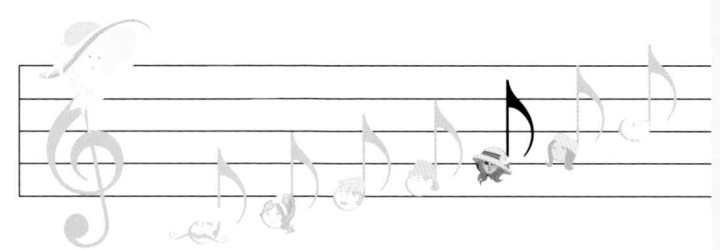

Gardener Grace
puts plants in place.
Her thumb is green.
She's Garden Queen.

When work is done,
she sings for fun.
We all agree
her note is "G."

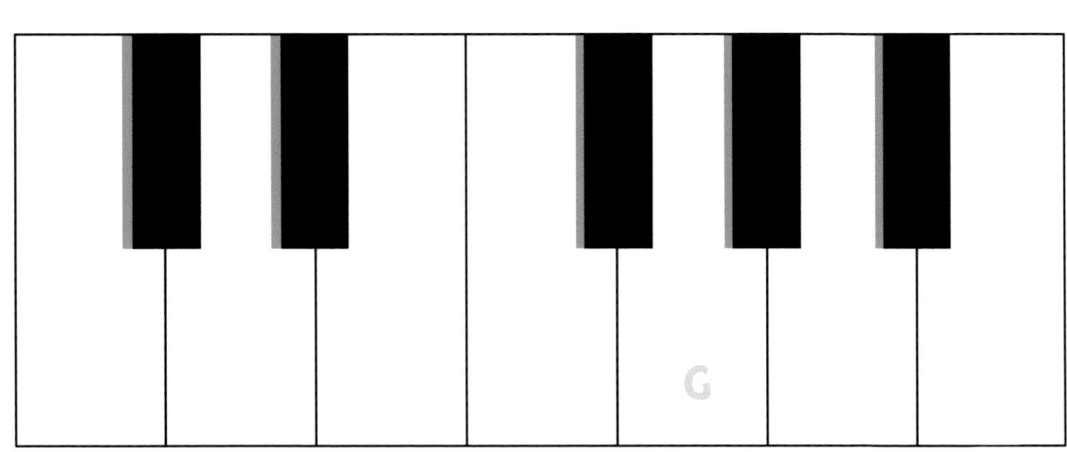

Hum "G" and stick the note on the right key!

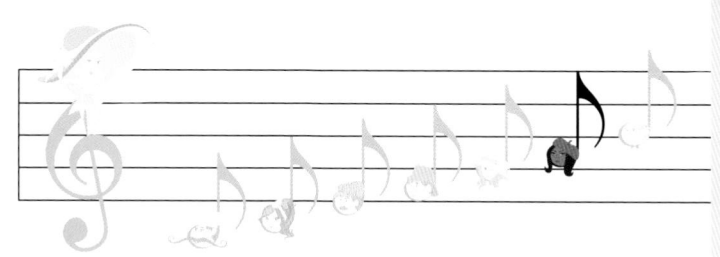

Abby the Artist
dresses the smartest.
She paints grins
and dimpled chins.

When work is done,
she sings for fun.
Time to play.
Her note is "A."

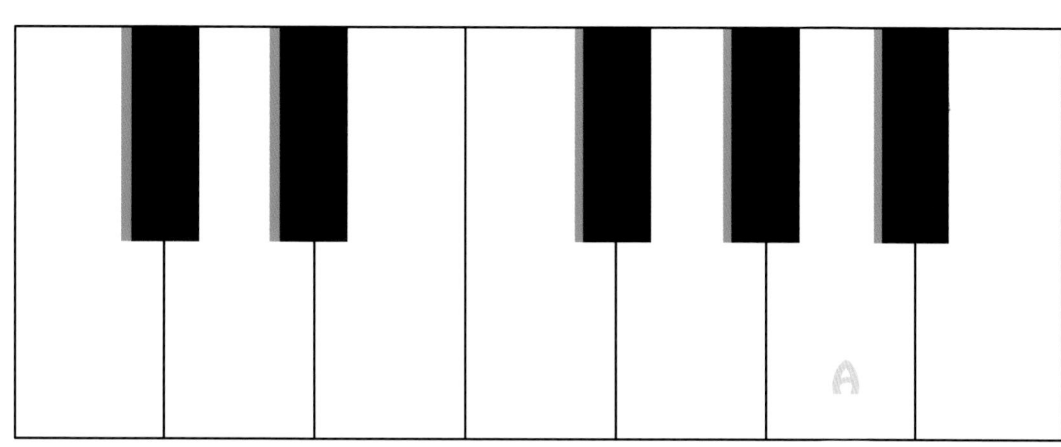

Hum "A" and stick the note on the right key!

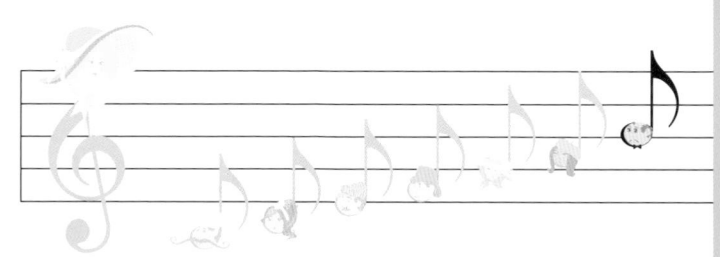

Butler Bobby
is slightly snobby.
He serves éclairs,
his nose in the air.

When work is done,
he sings for fun.
We all agree
his note is "B."

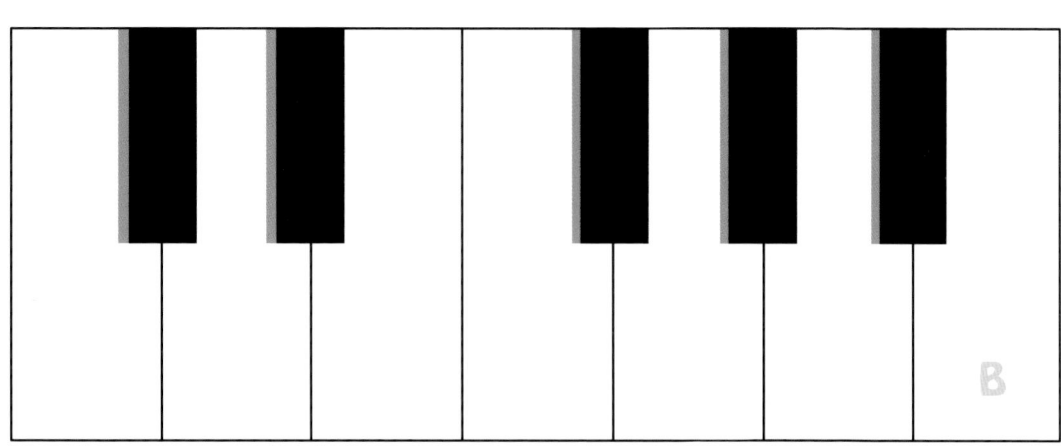

Hum "B" and stick the note on the right key!

The seven notes live in Treble Towers,
a friendly place filled with musical powers.
The notes each dwell on different floors
and hum and sing behind their doors.

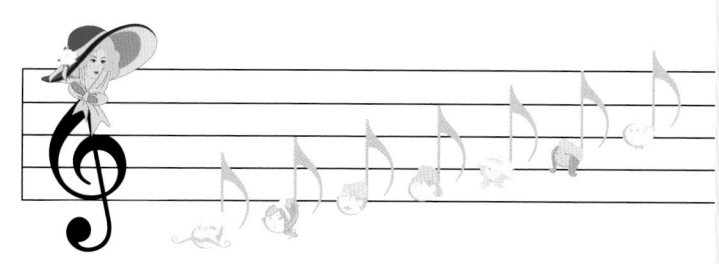

Lady Treble manages the Towers
in her big blue hat with the small white flowers.
The notes come home from work to play.
Oops! They can't get in today!

"We're in trouble!" the notes all shout.

"We've lost our keys and we're locked out.

We can't sing our Do Re Mi's.

Lady Treble, help us, please!"

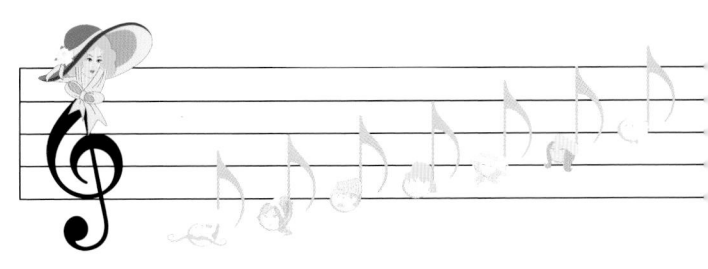

Lady Treble looks high and low,

from side to side, from head to toe.

Her hat blows off into the air.

"Aha!" she says. "They're in my hair!"

Now the notes each have a key.

They jump for joy and shout, "YIPPEE!"

They go inside and sing a song.

Use the stickers to play along.

**Hum all the notes and stick them on the staff
where they belong!**

Twinkle Twinkle Little Star

Twin - kle   twin - kle   lit - tle   star,   how   I   won - der   what   you   are!

Up   a - bove   the   world   so   high,   like   a   dia - mond   in   the   sky.

Twin - kle   twin - kle   lit - tle   star,   how   I   won - der   what   you   are!

Mary Had a Little Lamb

Ma - ry had - a   lit - tle   lamb,   lit - tle   lamb,   lit - tle   lamb!

Ma - ry had   a   lit - tle   lamb. Its   fleece was white as   snow!

Ev' - ry - where that   Ma - ry   went,   Ma - ry   went,   Ma - ry   went,

Ev' - ry - where that   Ma - ry   went, the   lamb was sure to   go!

Oh Susanna

Old Macdonald

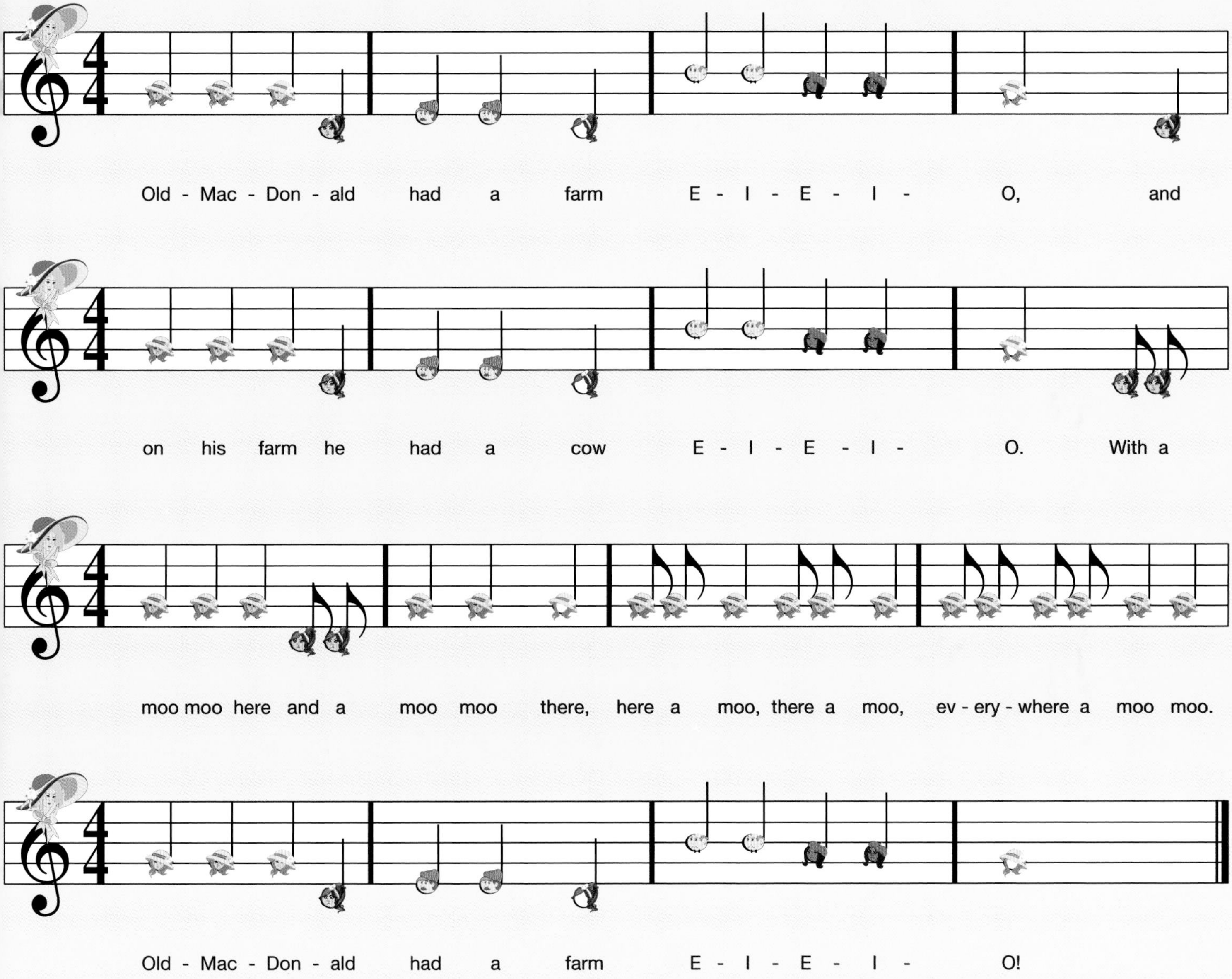

Old - Mac - Don - ald   had   a   farm   E - I - E - I -   O,   and

on   his   farm   he   had   a   cow   E - I - E - I -   O.   With a

moo moo here and a   moo moo   there,   here a   moo, there a   moo,   ev - ery - where a   moo moo.

Old - Mac - Don - ald   had   a   farm   E - I - E - I -   O!